Art by Maggie Clemmons
Coloring Book: Love Mandalas and Patterns
&
Happily Ever After: Stress Relieving
Coloring Book

1

You
are the poem
I never knew
how to write
and this life
is the story
I have always
wanted
to tell.

-Tyler Khott Gregson-

2

Contemporary Fiction by Susan McGeown:

Recipe for Disaster
Rules for Survival
A Well Behaved Woman's Life
The Butler Did It
Joining The Club
Embracing The Truth
The Best Secret (Coming)

Historical Fiction by Susan McGeown:

A Garden Walled Around Trilogy:
- Call Me Bear
- Call Me Elle
- Call Me Survivor

Rosamund's Bower
No Darkness So Great
Windermere Plantation

Nonfiction by Susan McGeown:

Biblical Women and Who They Hooked Up With
Biblical Warrior Women and Their Weapons
Jerusalem Times:
- JT: The Jesus of Nazareth Edition
- JT: The Twelve Apostles Edition

God's Phoenix Woman
The Rise of the Mighty (A Study of Acts)
What We Believe (A Study of Romans)
C.S. Lewis & Me
Old Testament 101
The Parables of Jesus
A Book of Thanks
Prayer & Me
A Book of Blessing
A Verse A Day.
Advice on Marriage, Love, and Friendship From Someone Who's Been There

ADVICE ON MARRIAGE, LOVE, AND FRIENDSHIP FROM SOMEONE WHO'S BEEN THERE

By Susan McGeown

Faith Inspired Books

Published by Faith Inspired Books

3 Kathleen Place, Bridgewater, New Jersey 08807

susanmcgeown@faithinspiredbooks.com

www.FaithInspiredBooks.com

Copyright September, 2019

All Rights Reserved

ISBN 13: 978-1-946268-06-8

ISBN 10- 1-946268-06-2

While certainly not a work of fiction, this book is most definitely a work of strong opinions! The advice, attitude, opinions, and observations as well as the shared statements, cartoons, quotes, and factual tidbits are all reflective of the author's strong personal beliefs about the importance of a biblical union between individuals. The author's opinions are not necessarily endorsed by the other contributors to this work and are wholly her own. Every effort has been made to be factually correct and provide as much bibliographic information as possible. Any mistakes are purely a result of the author's imperfections!!

For additions, deletions, corrections, or clarifications please contact Susan McGeown at the above address.

Bibliographic and footnote credit appears at the end of this work.

TO JOE & REBEKAH AMOROSA

In Honor and Celebration of their Marriage

November 17, 2019

AT WHICH THEY LET ME OFFICIATE!!!

WHOO-HOO!!!!

Two are better than one, because they have a good reward for their toil. For if they fall, one will lift up the other; but woe to one who is alone and falls and does not have another to help. Again, if two lie together, they keep warm; but how can one keep warm alone?
Ecclesiastes 4:9-11[3]

*Make my joy complete: be of the same mind, having the same love,
being in full accord and of one mind. Philippians 2:2*

TABLE OF CONTENTS

A NOTE FROM SUE

June 2019

This has been such a fun project to work on! It literally started as a simple letter to Joe and Rebekah thanking them for giving me the privilege of officiating their marriage. I was inspired to include in that letter my Top Ten Advice Tips for Marriage and … ended up with a book! Laugh Out Loud. Typical writer, I know.

As the book grew, I became intrigued with soliciting advice from others who had long term relationships. I initially sent out just a few emails to close family and friends and was so delighted with the responses, I sent out a global email. Finally, I just put it on my Facebook page and asked for advice from anyone who wanted to send it my way. They are scattered throughout and are identified

with a **bold, dark "box"** around each one. I hope you'll enjoy

reading these contributions as much as I did.

If you're like me, you tend not to pay much attention to footnotes in books. As I'm now a struggling seminary student, I have learned that footnotes are actually "the running conversation authors have with their readers" and have discovered fascinating comments, tips, and references that I otherwise would have previously ignored. Since I wanted to make this book an easy read with simple lists and fun pictures and comments, my author detailed dialogue (should you be interested in reading it) will appear in the back amidst the "Footnotes & Stuff" section. I hope this isn't too confusing.

I have always wanted, from the time I was a little girl, to get married and have a family. Even though I always knew I wanted to also be a teacher and a writer, the marriage and motherhood aspect has always been first and foremost. *And you need to know that I tried really hard to get married, too.* I was engaged not once, not twice, but three times before I met and married David (my hubby of 28+ years) and lest you think these were casual "pre-engagement" type engagements the last one was close enough that I already had The Dress, The Invitations were out, and had already had a bridal shower ...

I tell you this personal history because I need to tell you a story that came out of this. I initially spoke only to my mother about cancelling that wedding, not able to tell my father. He was a loving, supportive, encouraging Dad but for some reason I just couldn't face him with the news that I wasn't going to go through with the wedding scheduled less than six weeks away. I vividly remember him coming up to me the next morning and putting his hands on my shoulders and making me look at him. With tears in his eyes he said, "I've spoken with your mom and we both love you and are both proud of you. You need to know that you could be at the altar, in your big dress, and change your mind and I'd pick you up, carry you home, and that would be the end of it." This was that kind of love and support I grew up with as a child and the kind of marital relationship I so desperately wanted for myself.

From then on, it was a favorite story I liked to tell that perfectly epitomized my relationship with my mom and dad. So, fast forward a year and I am in a relationship that is rapidly headed for the altar. Dad, always a kidder, had grand fun in front of my intended by saying, "Remember: you can be in your big dress, and change your mind and I'll pick you up, carry you home, and that will be the end of it." To which David, all 6'4" of red-headed (joking) fury said, "TRY IT OLD MAN AND I'LL KNOCK YOU DOWN." Looking at me with an ear-to-ear grin and tears once again in his eyes, Daddy said in an emotion choked whisper, *"Now THAT'S what I was looking for!!"*

Marriage is not for the flighty or faint of heart. It's not for those who don't like to commit, are quick to throw in the towel, or are only looking for times filled with fun and laughter. There will be times that test your promises, there will be instances where you will want to run away and hide in a cave, and there will be moments of heartbreak and tears. But you see, marriage is a *joining.* It is literally a physical union that makes two completely separate individuals into one unified force. C.S. Lewis[4] says marriage is like a lock and a key; each is essential and valuable on its own but *together* they are always better and more useful. I really like that analogy.

Marriage has made me into the independent, outspoken, confident, strong, woman after God's own heart[5] that I am today. This is what I believe, regarding marriage (in no particular order):

1. I believe with all my heart that God has a Specially Chosen Perfect Person (if that is what one wants) out there for each one of us and if we can just follow His Lead, just be patient with His Timing, and just be obedient to His Instructions we will most definitely find the Specially Chosen Perfect Person.
2. I believe that marriage is an equal partnership in which its power is in the recognition of each other's strengths, the acceptance of each other's weaknesses, and the

encouragement of each other's growth, change, and maturity.

3. I believe that marriage is a monogamous union between two individuals who fully commit to a life plan in which both parties will be honored and appreciated.

4. I believe that marriage with a foundation in God's Purpose, Guidance, Love, Mercy, and Grace has a better potential for success and positive impact on the world than any other marital foundation possible.

5. I believe that marriage truly doubles all your life's joys and halves all your life's sorrows because there is always someone beside you either to hold you up or swing you around with joy.

6. And finally, I believe we are all unique, special, wanted, and called by God and that He can and will use us to His Glory and Benefit whether we are single or married, gay or straight, rich or poor, male, female, or transgender. (In case anyone was wondering!) 😊

With love,

Sue McGeown

I pray that God, the source of all hope, will fill you completely with joy and peace because you trust Him. Then you will overflow with confident hope through the power of the Holy Spirit. Romans 15:13

If you see the moon rising gently on your fields
If the wind blows softly on your face
If the sunset lingers
While the cathedral bells peal
And the moon has risen to her place

You can thank the Father for the things He has done
Thank Him for the things He's yet to do
And if you find a love that's tender
If you find someone who's true
Thank the Lord
He's been doubly good to you

If you look in the mirror at the end of a hard day
And you know in your heart you have not lied
If you gave love freely
If you earned an honest wage
And if you've got Jesus by your side

You can thank the Father for the things He has done
And thank Him for the things He's yet to do
And if you find a love that's tender
If you find someone who's true
Thank the Lord
He's been doubly good to you

Doubly Good by Amy Grant[6]

Set me as a seal upon your heart, as a seal upon your arm; for love is strong as death, passion fierce as the grave. Song of Solomon 8:6

TOP TEN ADVICE

1. **<u>Talk About The Important Stuff In Advance.</u>** Faith. Finances. Family. Friends. Remember compromise, unity, and love are key.
   - How will you handle the money? (Someone should probably take the lead...)
   - How will you handle the finances – for big purchases and small purchases?
   - What role do all these things play in your relationship?
   - Who, if anyone, will take the lead in certain areas of life?
   - What do you do in the case of an impasse?
   - Who do you trust?

- Who do you not trust?
- How will you deal with your (crazy?!?) extended family?
- Do you want children? How many?
- Who is going to be responsible for primary childcare?
- Whose job carries more clout when making life decisions?
- What are your future hopes and dreams?
- Where do you want to be in 5 years? 10 years? 15 years? 30 years? (Trust me, time flies. See the back of this book sections entitled "Do This Together" for more on this.)

2. **Don't Keep Score.** And, if you do keep score, keep it to yourself and remind yourself every time you think of the score that you shouldn't be keeping score! (Yes, I'm talking to myself.[7])

3. **Renew Your Promises Regularly.** Will you be my one and only? Will you love me forever? Will you stick with me through sickness and health, better and worse? (Why am I humming Meatloaf's 'Paradise By The Dashboard Lights'[8] all of a sudden?) Remember the promises you made when you were in your fanciest clothes and renew them regularly for when things are less than optimal. It keeps all these important commitments current and active.

4. **Happiness is Being Married To Your Best Friend.** Oh, that doesn't mean you don't have other essential friends, but what it does mean is that you (and everyone else) are fully aware who your #1 really is.

5. **Make Sure Each Other Always Comes First.** Yes, even once (if) those babies start happening, putting each other at the top of the priority list ensures a level of stability that cannot be shaken regardless of what you both will face.[9]

6. **<u>Recognize the Power of a Heartfelt Apology and the Importance of Sincere Forgiveness.</u>** An honest acknowledgement of a wrong done coupled with responsibility taken is often all anyone ever really wants or needs. Furthermore, you must understand that forgiveness isn't a weakness; it's one of the most difficult acts a person can do.

7. **<u>True Love's Proof Isn't Always What You Expect.</u>** It's not always flowery words, fancy cards, and cut flowers. It can be a love note taped inside the refrigerator, a heart drawn on your bathroom mirror with your good eyeliner, initials cut into the grass with the lawnmower, a note scribbled on the train and left under your pillow, half of a favorite candy bar left just for you, or even a favorite mug of tea sitting and ready for when you first wake up in the morning … you get the picture. These things show *I know you, I love you, I think of you, I'm glad your mine…*

8. **<u>Have a Top Three.</u>** What three things eclipse everything else in your life? Those three things will color literally everything else. Make sure that everyone who knows you, loves you, and cares about you know what your Top Three are. They shouldn't be a mystery or a secret! Here are mine:

> #1) My Faith Journey,
>
> #2) My Family, and
>
> #3) My Friends.

9. <u>**Don't Keep Secrets.**</u> There have been very few things that I have not discussed, shared, and sought advice on with David. *We don't always agree* but talking about it, coming up with a plan, and committing to be on the same page is absolutely essential to a solid relationship.[10] Even if the closest you can get is to, "agree to disagree" and decide who has the most invested to make the final decision! There are also some very important subcategories:
   a. Not being too proud to acknowledge mistakes made and change course, and
   b. Not saying, "I told you so" and being open and willing to repair resulting disasters from wrong decisions.

10. <u>**Speak The Truth.**</u> Trust and integrity will keep love alive and thriving. Treasure honesty. Value conversation. Don't squander precious moments. Once lost, they are almost impossible to reclaim.

Because things don't always go right, I'm so glad I have you on my left.

What I Believe Is Needed
To Be Married With Love
For Life:

Respect

Communicate

Readjust

Balance

Celebrate

Affection

Peg Amorosa[11]

Let all that you do be done in love. I Corinthians 16:14

HOW TO AVOID SLEEPING ON THE COUCH TOO OFTEN

"ARE YOU AGREEING WITH ME JUST TO SHUT ME UP?"

The Lockhorns[12]

1. **Don't Be Afraid...** To cry. To talk. To ask questions. To admit you're worried or need help. Staying silent and stoic is often the stupidest thing we humans like to do.[13]

2. **Don't Compare.** You are absolutely unique and that means your relationship is absolutely unique. You have no idea what anyone else's life entails. Be the best you can be and everything else will work itself out.

3. **Don't Go To Bed Angry.** And, when you do anyway, commit to fixing things in the light of dawn ASAP even if it just means bringing someone a hot cup of tea in bed.

4. **It's Okay to Be Wrong.** (Remember this especially if you are regularly always right...which immediately confirms that you're wrong in case you don't know...)

5. **Embrace Change.** Change is growth and growth is life. Find your own pace for progress and keep moving forward. This means changing attitudes, perceptions, and standards over time.

6. **Learn What Matters.** Each of you will have things you care about ... and things you don't. Be willing to adapt.

7. **Learn Your Weaknesses and Admit Them.** We're all good at some things but none of us are good at everything. (And if you think you are, please see #4, above.)

8. **Learn To Laugh At Yourself.** That way you will never take yourself too seriously which is a perfect recipe for disaster.

9. **When In Doubt, Don't Say It.** At least wait twenty-four hours before you say it or text it.

10. **Learn to Prioritize.** House and yard work are only top priorities if you both want them to be important.

11. **Count To Ten.** Take the time to organize your thoughts (and maybe cool down?) before saying or writing/sending something.[14]

12. **Which Side?** Please remember that there are always three sides to every situation: your side, your partner's side, and reality.

13. **Trade shoes.** Not literally. But my son the lawyer has this excellent technique where he puts himself in the opposing side of the issue and tries to defend a point from that

perspective … in anticipation of how *he* plans to argue his actual point. (A little like tying your shoes in the mirror, I know!) A number of times, looking at family drama situations from this perspective has really helped in compromise, understanding, apologies, and forgiveness.

14. **<u>Being On Different Pages Isn't All Bad.</u>** They say you are often attracted to your opposite. I prefer to say you are often drawn to *what compliments* you. Let's face it, if you have almost no common ground (except the bedroom) to stand on then this relationship doesn't have much promise! But different perspectives are an opportunity to learn and grow. Don't be afraid to add another page to your play book every now and then.

LOVE
is patient
is kind
it does not envy
it does not boast
it is not proud
it is not rude
it is not self-seeking
it is not easily angered
keeps no record of wrongs
does not delight in evil
rejoices with the truth
always protects
always trusts
always hopes
always perseveres
never fails

1 Corinthians 13:4-8a

I Corinthians 13:4-8a

My mom always told me "you'll just know" .... and she was right.
I knew my guy was the one on that first date.

The person you marry should be someone you love ... who is your friend ... who you trust 100%. Someone who you frequently agree with, but who, when you disagree, respects your point of view. Respect theirs.

Give each other freedom, respect, companionship, encouragement, understanding, time alone ...

Be there for each other.... through good times and bad times .... be prepared for the unexpected .... for it will happen....

Forgive and allow yourself to be forgiven ... remember to notice the little things ... they are bigger than you know ... have faith in God and each other ... Amen.

Francine Giorello[15]

SPIRITUAL ADVICE YOU REALLY NEED TO TAKE TO HEART

FAITH
(F) FORWARDING
(A) ALL
(I) ISSUES
(T) TO
(H) HEAVEN

1. **Learn To Pray About Things.** That may not mean that you spend hours together on your knees but it does mean that no life decision, no matter how big or small, is done without prayerful conversation with Your Lord. (I Thessalonians 5:17[16])

2. **Learn to Believe (and Trust) That God Will Guide You.** My gut is where I personally get direct messages and guidance from God. Seriously. If my gut is all tense and twisted, I've learned it means I'm way off track on something and need to reevaluate and readjust things via serious prayer and careful thought. (Proverbs 3:5-6[17])

3. **Commit Your Plans To God.** Determine that wherever you go your goal driven purpose is to make God smile and follow His plans for your life.[18] (Jeremiah 29:11[19])

4. **Embrace Big Black Arrows.** Recognize that you cannot control your life; no matter how hard you try. I'm rather clueless and preoccupied with my busy life so I always ask for God's Guidance in the form of Big, Black, Arrows: "Please paint a big, black, arrow on the ground, Lord, and I'll happily follow it." (Caution: BBA's can come in all shapes and sizes but are *always* by the Lord's Love and Design[20].) (Proverbs 19:21[21])

5. **Recognize Your Blessings.** God's blessings must be acknowledged, appreciated, and praised. Remember, all good things come from God. (Romans 8:28[22])

6. **Become a Friend of God.** Don't be a stranger. Determine to figure out what all this spiritual stuff is all about. Start by reading the Bible. Favorite books of mine are Philippians, Romans, and the Gospel of Luke. And a list of my most favorite Bible verses are in the back of this book, too. (James 2:23[23])

7. **Find A Translation Of The Bible You Like.** No, that doesn't mean you have to buy thirty-five different translations and read each one of them! Go on www.biblegateway.com and look up a few of my favorite Bible verses (those are in the back of this booklet and that's, of course, before you follow through and look up the entire list). Which one do you like best? Which one speaks to you most clearly. Popular translation favorites of mine are also listed in the back. (Psalm 119:105[24])

8. **Find a Church Family.** Don't expect perfection or all the answers. Do expect love, fellowship, support, encouragement, and belonging. Don't settle. Keep looking until you find the perfect spot that feels like home. (Matthew 18:20[25])

9. **Love Like You Want To Be Loved.** Patience, kindness, gentleness, self-control, goodness, faithfulness... You won't get what you aren't willing to give. (Galatians 5:22-23[26])

10. **Have a spiritual anchor.** This is someone you trust and can reach out to. It will keep things in perspective: a Bible study group, a trusted spiritual friend, a minister of your choice... (Luke 6:47-49[27])

"**Each of the Fruits of the Spirit is but a Phase of Love:**

- **Joy** is love exulting.
- **Peace** is love reposing.
- **Patience** is love enduring.
- **Goodness** is the good manners of love.
- **Kindness** is love in action.
- **Faithfulness** is love confiding.
- **Gentleness** is love yielding.
- **Self-Control** is true self-love."

A. W. Tozer

A.W. Tozer[28]

11. **Ask Questions.** Find a spiritual person you respect and trust and ask them some questions. No one has all the answers, but sometimes good conversation generates all kinds of growth and discovery. Someone with a precious faith should be more than willing to share what they believe, why they believe, what they struggle with (of course they do!), what they wonder about, what were their most precious spiritual moments (these are usually really, really cool...) (Matthew 7:7[29])

12. **Stay Close to God**. Especially when things are good! Especially when things are running smoothly! Remember to be thankful when things are good! (What? You're surprised at this advice? I don't have to tell you to get close to God when things go south... Almost everyone always "gets close to God" when things are bad...) (Psalm 63:7[30])

13. **Have a moral anchor**. Determine what matters, what's worth fighting for, and what's worth not fighting for. Without one, you are completely and utterly adrift. (Psalm 106:3[31])

14. **Learn to be Thankful**. We tend to forget that "Whatever is good and perfect is a gift coming down to us from God our Father, who created all the lights in the heavens. He never changes or casts a shifting shadow."[32] I firmly believe that until you acknowledge what God has already blessed you with, you won't be able to appreciate anything more... Understanding that you are never alone, that God has gone before you to prepare things, and then taking the time to be thankful for *what goodness you can*

acknowledge in the midst of disaster is a powerful coping mechanism..[33]

15. **Read Some Quality God Stuff**. Current favorites for me are: (Proverbs 1:7[34])

> 1.) The Purpose Driven Life by Rick Warren[35],
>
> 2.) My Utmost For His Highest by Oswald Chambers[36],
>
> 3.) Mere Christianity by C.S. Lewis[37],
>
> 4.) The Reason For God by Tim Keller [38],
>
> 5.) Mornings With The Holy Spirit by Jennifer LeClaire[39],
>
> 6.) The Four Vision Quests of Jesus by Steven Charleston[40],
>
> 7.) Jesus and The Disinherited by Howard Thurman[41],
>
> 8.) The Pursuit of God by A. W. Tozer[42],
>
> 9.) Half The Church by Carolyn Custis James[43],
>
> 10.) Women of the Bible by Ann Spangler & Jean E. Syswerda[44],
>
> 11.) Prayer: Does It Make Any Difference? by Philip Yancey[45]
>
> 12.) The Prodigal God by Tim Keller [46]
>
> 13.) Jesus Unbound by Keith Giles[47]

GOD'S 3 ANSWERS TO YOUR PRAYERS:

1. YES.
2. NOT YET.
3. I HAVE SOMETHING BETTER IN MIND.

Always tell the truth.

Marylynn Oudheusden[48]

Don't keep score.

Herb Oudheusden

I have no greater joy than this, to hear that my children are walking in the truth. 3 John 4

ADVICE ON KIDS (OR CHILDISH ADULTS)[49]

Jem S[50]

1. **Fighting.** Do it in private. Don't ever enlist the kids to take sides. Always take the high road and be exemplary in your behavior because where you screw up is what they will remember most.

2. **Discuss Stuff In Advance.** One of you will invariably be the worrier and one of you will invariably be the optimist. Learn to discuss worries before they happen so when

things hit the fan (and oh, they will, trust me) you will already have a vague plan in place. (Once David and I had teenagers, we actually role played potential discussions...!)

3. **Pay Attention.** "I hate school," says your kid in passing for the first time in forever but won't say anything else no matter how hard you try to get them to talk. "Joe and I aren't friends anymore," says your kid who's been friends with Joe since they were in diapers. That might be the only glimpse you get, but be thankful for it and do some digging. Contact those teachers or counselors or even reliable (note that word "reliable" please) parents and ask a few questions.

4. **Make Your Home A Haven.** Nothing makes me happier than 16 pairs of giant, smelly sneakers piled in my front hallway, the television blasting the latest playoff game, and potato chips ground into the carpet. Be the parent that's always willing to chaperone, host, transport, bake, organize... They will be gone sooner than you ever imagined and you'll be oh-so glad you spent those eight hours on your only free Saturday judging the debate team.

5. **Make Lemonade Out Of Lemons.** (Although I regularly mix this up and say, "Make Lemons out of Lemonade" which makes people look at me strangely so I say, "Oh, you know what I mean!") This was a skill my husband had to teach me. Such as when your teen tells you at 11:45 p.m. that he needs to be transported 45 minutes away and be somewhere by 7 a.m. the next morning (also on your only free Saturday). Instead of getting furious (although you can discuss better advanced planning or consequences in the future) drop the annoying child off and go to

breakfast and to your favorite plant store to add something to your garden. (Make it a date!![51])

6. **Have Good Rules.** Fair ones. Realistic ones. Ones that you actually discuss and explain (and hopefully agree on) with your child. Ones that you model as well.

7. **Have Good Consequences.** Let's face it if you take away their phone, all social media, and ground them for life you've cashed in all your chips. What are you going to do if something happens again? And, more importantly, *what does your kid have to lose if he or she decide to get in trouble again?*[52]

8. **Have Good Rewards.** Your kid is as reliable as clockwork: they are never late when given a curfew or a deadline. Acknowledge that! Reward that!

Picture by Eloise Wilkin[53]

9. **Fair Doesn't Always Mean Same.** We learned this the hard way, so you'll just have to trust me on this. You have one kid that has earned the privilege of a cell phone (good grades, good homework performance, does chores when asked around the house). You have another kid who you're determined won't have a cell phone until they move out and buy one for themselves. Trouble is, only one child is reachable by you when they are out of the house and yet they have multiple ways to communicate with friends through other various means. How does that work for you? Not very well, trust me. Remember, you are in charge, you set the rules. Make sure rules work for you and not against you.

10. **Teach Them The Value Of Money Early.** They are never too young to start understanding saving, sharing, tithing (that's a church thing!!), and spending wisely. Trust me, nothing is more appreciated and cared for that has been worked for, saved for, and bought with their "own money."

11. **Read To Your Kids.** Make it a habit that becomes a fond memory. You will establish a valuable routine for life.

12. **Play With Your Kids.** Video games, basketball, Legos, dolls, coloring, crafting...*spend precious time with them.* It doesn't have to be days or hours, it just has to be one on one memorable, loving time. (AND PUT YOUR PHONE AWAY.)

Bil Keane [54]

13. **<u>Don't Be Perfect.</u>** When you make a mistake, when appropriate and possible, share it with your child. Explain what happened, why it was a mistake, and the consequences you faced as a result. Setting yourself up to be infallible isn't realistic (and trust me, at some point they'll know you've been scamming them anyway).

14. **<u>Be Prepared To Fail.</u>** It. Will. Happen. Sometimes. That's why modeling good choices even when you mess up (See Above) is good.

15. **<u>Sometimes It's Good To Miss Someone.</u>** Take a break sometimes. You can't be with someone you love 24/7. I learned that when I had three babies under 5 and couldn't wait to get out of the house only to discover once I was wandering around aimlessly in the mall that I couldn't wait to get home and see my babies...[55]

16. **Always Remember.** You are not PARTICIPATING IN a fight. As a parent, you must always be ONLY THE REFEREE. The referee never joins the fight, right?

17. **There's Never A Perfect Time.** To have a baby. There will always be something hanging fire that you want to solve or get done … trust me. And once that little bundle arrives, you'll be amazed how your entire list of priorities shifts, too.

18. **Appreciate Advice But Remember You Have A Brain.** Some advice (like never disturb a contented baby even if she is just sucking on her toes) is invaluable. Other advice may be questionable. Listen politely, ask any questions you may have, and then use your common sense. If the advice doesn't easily fit into your life or routine, forget it or adapt it.

Someecards[56]

RESPECT is the key. Treat others the way you want to be treated. If you can't say something nice, don't say anything at all. Be the person who gives the compliment that makes someone's day.

Melanie Young[57]

Therefore encourage one another and build up each other...
I Thessalonians 5:11

ON FRIENDS

Baby Blues by Rick Kirkman and Jerry Scott[58]

1. **Friends and Your Significant Other** – Your significant other should never feel that they are not as loved/wanted/respected/valued as much as any other relationship outside your marriage. Your significant other may not understand exactly what you see in certain close friends that you have, but they should never feel threatened by another relationship.[59]

2. **Friends and The Real You** – The 'real you' that is the person that is deep down in the core of your being shouldn't just come out when you're with one person or another. The Real You should be evident at all times to the people who know and care about you (okay, maybe the "Real You" is louder with certain people but still...). If you "go out and get crazy" with just one friend then you

need to evaluate the person you are at other times. Who is the real you and why do you need multiple faces?

3. **Friends and Life** – Friends should
   a.) <u>Enrich the quality of your life</u> – Is their influence positive and appropriate?
   b.) <u>Challenge you and make you think</u> – Do they bring up perspectives that cause you to think and better understand your own thoughts?
   c.) <u>Be honest.</u> – Can you count on them to tell you truthfully what you are trying to find out (even if it's a tough topic)?
   c.) <u>Know how to keep secrets.</u> – Are you confident that your private discussions (unless your safety is a concern) are kept private?
   d.) <u>Avoid "Triangle Conversations."</u> That means that your Friend A doesn't talk trash about you when they are with Friend B and you are not present. And, if they do this about other friends *to you*, you can be sure they are doing it elsewhere *about you*.
   e.) <u>Listen.</u> Can you be honest about your feelings, concerns, and challenges or do you have to be 'a different person' when you're with these 'friends'?
   f. <u>Strengthen.</u> Are you confident when you are with this friend that the person you are is better/stronger/wiser?

4. **Friends are a Reflection of Who You Are**. Your friends might not all be alike (or maybe they are – what do they have in common?) but they are a definite indicator of the type of person you are. "The one consistent feature of all your dissatisfying relationships is you.[60]"

5. **Some Friendships End**. It's happened to me just a very few times but it has been a devastating break. Whether you initiated it or they did, sometimes the best thing that can happen for you both to go your separate ways. Remember, God brings people *into your life* but He also might take people *out of your life*. If you are faced with compromising your core principals or maintaining a friendship, you're always better off staying true to what you know is right. A.L.W.A.Y.S.

6. **Friendships Can Happen At Any Time**. Yes, we have lifelong friends (the ones that have been with us through thick and thin) but there are always new opportunities out there. Don't isolate yourself.

If you know what you bring to the table, you'll never be afraid to eat alone.

Not sure what to say after 50 years, only that I made a commitment to Carl and God. Marriage has its ups, downs, and transitions. Going through the hard times made me a stronger person, most importantly it made me rely on God. The good times reinforced us to keep building our relationship. Love and friendship keep us together. I have always had a strong belief that God planned for us to meet and marry and He has seen us through the journey.

Kris Weigner[61]

But wisdom from above is first pure, then peaceable, gentle,
willing to yield, full of mercy and good fruits,
without a trace of partiality or hypocrisy. James 3:17

ADVICE I WASN'T GOING TO PUT IN, BUT DECIDED TO ANYWAY

GLASBERGEN

"Don't wash off this hand stamp. You may need it later
if you leave your marriage and want to get back in."

Randy Glasbergen[62]

1. **Lying Isn't Always So Bad.** "Do I look fat?" "Isn't this fantastic?!" "Is this as bad as it looks?!" "Am I a failure?!" "Will I ever get this right?" Perhaps, eventually, at some time in the future, you can say, "Remember when you asked me..."and clarify or elaborate, but sometimes, saying the thing that will *comfort, encourage, or merely neutralize a volatile situation* is better then the cold, hard, stark truth. ("This meatloaf is disgusting. What are the hard crunchy things I keep chewing?"[63])

2. **Sometimes It Really Is The Thought That Counts.** You come home to a completely, totally, absolutely destroyed kitchen and babies wandering around who should already be in bed. You are led to a fancy meal on the good china with the good silver and candles flickering in the dining room. You'd prefer a spoon, jar of peanut butter, sleeping children, and a spotless kitchen. But you make yourself appreciate the effort and focus on that.[64]

3. **Therapy Helps.** Whether you go as a couple or as an individual, if you think you need it, by all means, GO. Find someone that you can like, respect, and trust and at least make sure that you are in the best place you can be to deal with things.[65]

4. **Be Thankful For Things That Aren't Always Thankworthy.** Well into parenting, I discovered that God often revealed some really horrible, mind-destroying things[66] to me *before* the proverbial you-know-what hit the fan. I realized, that this enabled me to: 1.) Scream, cry, and curse in private in my pillow for as long as I wanted. 2.) Pray. 3.) Talk to my trusted family member or friend and get advice. 4.) Appear amazingly calm, together, and

confident when dreaded fan moment actually hit. (I only realized this after a particularly nasty incident and someone complimented me on how I handled it all. I responded with an eyeroll and, "Oh, that's only because I found out about this 2 days ago. You should have seen me Friday!)

5. **Learn When To Say No.** Life gets really busy really fast. Remember that *quality* is much more important than *quantity* and if adding the fourth after work responsibility is going to make everything else suffer you need to say, "NO." Trust me. Everyone (even the person you said no to) will be appreciative in the end.

6. **It's Not Always Your Job.** Learn when to let things go … and, yes, sometimes fail spectacularly. Sometimes that's the only way people learn (children AND adults). Let everyone know in advance that you live to say, "I told you so!"[67] (Yes, that's me.)

7. **Don't Be Afraid to Change An Opinion.** Conversation, discussion, questions, research, prayer, debate, and personal thought should lead you to a better place. Maybe, what you thought was a good thought turned out to be not so good as you thought. Think about that.

8. **Video Games Aren't All Bad.** David and I spent many enjoyable months working on the computer game *Myst*[68] together. (This was definitely before kids!!) *And* I lost months of my life playing *Zelda: Ocarina of Time*[69] with my then 5-year-old son (and refused to start playing another one because it was soooo fun but sooooo time consuming!). Both of these experiences provided

interesting insight into the person I gamed with that I don't believe I would have gained in any other venue.

9. **There Are Many Different Ways to Say Love; Learn Which One Your Partner Wants To Hear.** If your love likes breakfast in bed, make the breakfast! But if your love's favorite morning sound is to wake up to the sound of the dishwasher being emptied then ...[70]

Sorrow Looks Back
Worry Looks Around
Faith Looks Up

I have three pieces of life advice I give to "about to be married" and "married expecting kids" couples:

1) (Up to the start of the wedding ceremony itself): It's never, ever too late to call the wedding off.
2) Everything that comes out of a child will wash off. It may stain, but it will wash off.
3) (Importantly) Unsolicited advice (even mine; especially mine) is pretty worthless.

my story and sticking to it,
Tom Vaden[71]

A friend loves at all times... Proverbs 17:17a

THEMS FIGHTING RULES

Sandra Boynton[72]

TOP Things Couples Fight About[73]

- Money
- Family Communication
- Children
- Intimacy
- Time
- Priorities
- Jealousy

- Religion
- Politics
- The Past
- Chores/Responsibilities
- Romance
- Pet-Peeves
- In-laws

1. **Arguments Aren't Always Bad.** Believe it or not, arguments, *if they are productive and lead to learning, growth, and positive change* are actually quite beneficial. It's better to argue and learn than keep it all bottled up and become a human volcano.

2. **Walking Away.** If you're going to lose control and say something you know you will regret, walk away. I'm moody and often can't articulate adequately what's bothering me. I need to be given some time to cool down and organize my thoughts into a rational, cohesive sentence or two. Or five. Or twenty-seven...

3. **Fairness.** I know it's tough, but try to fight fair. Don't say things you know are going to trigger Hiroshima and don't bring up past issues that have (or haven't) been resolved which will only complicate matters.

4. **Somethings Are Better Left Unsaid.** Words can't be taken back. Comments can live longer than you. If you're only goal is to cause pain or hurt, keep your dang mouth shut.

5. **Fight Straight.** Are you tired? Tense? Hungover? Loaded? Or is your partner? Finding the right time to talk about something is half the battle to a successful ... discussion (I was going to say fight but I changed my mind).

CRAZY Things Couples Seriously Fight About[74]

- What to eat for dinner
- Driving habits
- Picking a movie or t.v. show to watch
- How long to stay out when you're out

- How to load the dishwasher
- Leaving drawers/cabinets open
- Drying hands on decorative towels
- Doing laundry
- Sleep habits
- Changing the toilet roll
- Leaving the toilet seat up
- Being too honest
- Spending money 'foolishly'
- Being unenthusiastic over a gift
- Not paying attention when having a conversation
- Farting
- Talking trash about friends/family
- The thermostat
- Dirty laundry on the floor
- Doing the dishes
- Planning
- Holidays
- Lost keys/phone/headphones, etc.
- Insincere apologies
- Fighting over the same thing repeatedly

I'm not arguing.

I'm simply explaining why I'm right.

"Marriage is like a triangle with God on top and the husband and wife below. The closer a husband or wife gets to God, the shorter the distance between them."

Todd Buurstra[75]

"Choose the battle, most of the things you fight about are not important. Then, let it go."

Natsuko Buurstra[76]

...I found him whom my soul loves. I held him, and would not let him go... Song of Solomon 3:4

INTERESTING MARRIAGE TIDBITS MAYBE YOU DIDN'T KNOW...

1. There is **no actual, formal marriage ceremony in the Bible**. There are verses in Genesis that epitomize God's plan for a union of the first two humans in the Garden of Eden but the traditional wedding ceremony that most of us are familiar with is not in the Bible, anywhere.[77] And, just to completely blow your mind, you need to know that there is *no formal Hebrew term* that specifically means only "wife" or only "husband" in the Bible either.[78]

2. **A Biblical Union** is done *in God's presence and is mindful and desirous of God's blessing and guidance* and is to have these specific qualities (I'm just looking at Genesis 2:24[79]):
a.) A Unity of Individuals – we're talking a serious joining, staying, sticking closely together,[80]
b.) A Priority Between Individuals – that means that aside from your spiritual commitment with God there is nothing (I'm talking absolutely *no-thing*) that has a greater importance than your chosen partner,[81]
c.) A Lifetime Commitment of Individuals – this decision that both individuals decide to enter into is literally the

creation of a new entity. A transformation if you will which *cannot be undone.*[82]

3. **Perks of a Biblical Union** include (Now I'm looking at Genesis 1:28)[83] God's blessing[84] of this union which causes the recipients to:
a.) <u>Be fruitful and multiply</u> - which means exactly what you think it means – SEX – and why partaking in the act of sexual intercourse with someone is a *very* serious step toward the commitment department and should never be engaged in cavalierly.
b.) <u>Have children or produce something bigger than just themselves</u> – choosing to not have children or being unable to have children does not in any way mean that an individual – and *especially a biblically married couple* cannot be positively influential and promoting God's plan for this world.[85]
c.) <u>Be Stewards of the Earth</u> – which implies a power and superiority *as well as* a vast responsibility to always *do what is pleasing to God.*[86]

4. **Jesus** talked about very little about marriage, divorce, and adultery, however, when he did, he spoke of it very seriously. Matthew 19:1-12, Mark 10:1-12, and John 8:1-11 are the main passages where he addresses these subjects directly.[87] A careful reading of these passages (they're in the footnotes if you're curious) will show that Jesus did not, in any way, contradict God's union of the first humans. His main points regarding a biblical union between individuals are:
a.) <u>Marriage</u> is absolutely seriousness regarding unity, priorities, and lifetime commitments,

b.) Some of <u>Moses' rules</u> regarding marriage/divorce were put in place because of humanity's faults and not by God's design,

c.) <u>Marriage</u> is not meant for all of humanity,

d.) Producing <u>children</u> is not meant for all of humanity,

e.) <u>No human</u> is perfect,

f.) <u>Love, mercy, grace, and forgiveness</u> are always superior to punishment and condemnation.

5. **Marriage and Equality.** Don't let anyone tell you that women are subordinate to men or wives are subordinate to husbands.

   <u>God ordained equality</u>: Genesis 5:2 *Male and female He created them, and He blessed them and named them "adam" when they were created.* At creation, God made NO DISTINCTION between male and female humans. He consistently calls on, uses, and empowers women throughout the Old Testament.

   <u>Jesus modeled equality</u>: Find an example *anywhere* in scripture that He does not! His parables reflect women as equal, his entourage reflects women as equal, his ministry reflects women as equal, his final moments reflect women as equal, and his Great Commission[88] reflects women as equal.

   <u>The Holy Spirit empowered with equality</u>[89]: Acts chapters 1-2 clearly record the presence of women as part of the group of believers who were "constantly devoting themselves to prayer...[90]" The New Testament is filled with examples of women being empowered by the Holy Spirit.

   <u>Paul taught equality</u>: Ephesians 5:21 *Be subject to one another out of reverence for Christ* (always read that *entire*

passage of Ephesians 5:21-33[91] *and* if anyone ever tries to quote you the verse about wives "being subject" to their husbands – v. 22, make sure you point out that also in the passage it is only *husbands* are directed to love their wives – v.33) and Galatians 3:28 *There is no longer Jew or Greek, there is no longer slave or free, there is no longer male and female; for all of you are one in Christ Jesus.*

6. **Wedding rings** are traditionally worn on the 4th finger of the left hand because long ago it was believed that there was a vein in the hand in that specific finger that traveled directly to the heart. However, if you travel to Europe even today, many married couples wear their rings on the ring finger of the *right hand!* And, originally, only women wore the rings.

7. The saying *used to be* **"Something old, something new, something borrowed, something blue, and a sixpence in your shoe."** Representing longevity (old), optimistic future (new), gaining "good luck" (you were supposed to borrow underwear from a fertile couple!!!) (borrowed), to deflect the Evil Eye as blue stood for love, purity and fidelity (blue), and prosperity (sixpence).

8. **Tie the Knot!!** Many cultures around the world even today actually *tie the hands of the bride and groom together* during the ceremony. And in the really olden days, when finding a priest/minister to marry you wasn't as easy as it is today or you weren't completely sure of your course of action, they used to practice "handfasting." Handfasting was sort of a trial marriage and lasted exactly a year and a day. After which you either formally married or separated.

9. The original **job of groomsman** was to help the groom kidnap the bride. This was during the popular trend of "marriage by capture" when a small army was needed to fight off angry relatives and help the groom escape with his intended.

10. The original **job of the bridesmaid** was to dress exactly like the bride in order to confuse the evil spirits and protect her from being identified and potentially cursed.

11. **The groom always stands to the bride's right** so that his right hand – or his sword hand – is free to fight/defend against a jealous rival. If you're disagreeing with this, you're probably Jewish as their tradition is exactly the opposite.

12. **Throwing the bride's garter** came about from the ancient practice of tearing off a part of the bride's gown as a token of good luck. That's why she **throws her bouquet**, too.

13. Speaking of **bridal bouquets**, originally their purpose was to smell very strongly to ward off evil spirits and to mask the unpleasant scent of body odor.

14. In some cultures, **the top of the wedding cake** is set aside and saved for either the first anniversary or the birth or christening of the couple's first child (whichever comes first). This was done for our blessing in England and they didn't even freeze it! (Wedding cakes in the UK are often fruit cakes which are then "hermetically sealed" with marzipan icing.)

15. **Carrying the bride over the threshold** harks back to the time when it was worried that the new bride would track

in evil spirits to the groom's home. This was the safest way to avoid this issue, apparently.

16. **Richard Wagner's "Bridal Chorus"** better known as "Here Comes the Bride" was the wedding anthem after 1858 when it made its first appearance in a British royal wedding[92].

17. **Posting Banns of Marriage** was originally a proclamation or public announcement in a church or the town council of an impending marriage between two persons. It was to enable anyone to raise any canonical or civil legal impediment to the marriage, so as to prevent marriages that would be invalid. Up until 1983 the Roman Catholic Church required this and in many Catholic countries they still are published!

18. **Tying Cans on the back of cars** is from the old custom of throwing a "charivari" for the couple – a celebration in which neighbors would walk down the streets and bang their pots and pans to make as much noise as possible throughout the village in order to scare away evil spirits.

19. **Wedding Cakes** were originally symbols of fertility and the couple was challenged to kiss over the top of the cake without knocking it over for good fortune. That's why they grew to multiple layers – to make it tougher!!

THE SECRET TO LONG-TERM RELATIONSHIPS.

Cathy Thorne[93]

We do stuff we like to do apart and it's OK. I love concerts but John hates loud music. Therefore, I attend many shows with other friends and family, and come home to tell him all about it.

John loves to fish up in New Hampshire and the boat goes far out in the ocean for hours and hours. Absolutely not my cup of tea. So likewise, he goes on fishing trips and comes home to tell me all about it. Plus with delicious fish!!

Win-Win!

There is absolutely no reason couples should do everything together if both don't love the activity. Why make the other person suffer?

We do both like going to movies and comedy shows, going down the shore, eating out and walking in the park, so we do that stuff together.

Sue Betz[94]

How precious to me are your thoughts, O God!
How vast is the sum of them! Psalm 139:17

DO THIS TOGETHER: QUICK RESPONSES

You can fill this in or just use it as a starting point for interesting discussions. (HOWEVER, if you write your answers down and save them, it might be fun to see how things change year to year...)

	ME	YOU
First thing I liked about you		

	ME	YOU
I knew we were destined to be together when...		
Something you've taught me already...		
Favorite moment so far with you...		

	ME	YOU
Best thing you've ever said to me...		
Funniest moment with you...		
Favorite place to be with you...		

	ME	YOU
I can't believe you actually...		
Current obsession...		
Do you think you'll ever...		

	ME	YOU
Remember when we…		
One thing I know you absolutely can't stand…		
Something said about you that you didn't know was said…		

	ME	YOU
I always imagined I'd end up with someone who…		
One of these days, I'm going to get you to…		
I know I will never get you to…		

	ME	YOU
The best way to cheer you up is to...		
The favorite thing I do for you is...		
I really, _really_ love you when you...		

-Don't go into a marriage with an escape plan(divorce). It is too easy to use it when things aren't perfect. If you go into marriage KNOWING that it is for life, truly for life, then your mind set is different. It also gives you freedom. You have the freedom to be yourself, your best self as well as your worst self. It gives your partner the same opportunity. By being able to not have to always have your best face on you are not only reducing stress but you are also allowing yourself, and your partner, the opportunity for self -reflection and growth.

-Marriage is not always wonderful. It is a journey. Journeys are always changing. Sometimes they are fun, sometimes sad. Sometimes they are easy, sometimes hard. Sometimes they are exciting, sometimes boring but they are always changing.

-Do activities with other people. Don't do everything with your partner but make sure you do do some things together.

Robin Casucci[95]

And my God will fully satisfy every need of yours according to his riches in glory in Christ Jesus. Philippians 4:19

DO THIS TOGETHER: THINGS WE HAVE TO HAVE

Henry Payne[96]

Think: Home, profession, personal time, hobbies, vacations, health insurance, medical health, church/spiritual involvement, money, family relationships, geographic location... These are practical, realistic, "I can sleep peacefully at night" things that you both agree on and pray for and work toward.[97]

PROFESSIONALLY:

Immediately	
5 years	
10 years	
25 years	
Retirement	

RELATIONSHIP-WISE:

Immediately	
5 years	
10 years	
25 years	
Retirement	

Happiness is being married to your best friend.

Renew your vows every day.

Submit completely to your wife at all times.

David McGeown[98]

"Therefore I tell you, do not be anxious about your life, what you will eat or what you will drink, nor about your body, what you will put on. Is not life more than food, and the body more than clothing? ²⁶ Look at the birds of the air: they neither sow nor reap nor gather into barns, and yet your heavenly Father feeds them. Are you not of more value than they?" Matthew 6:25-26

DO THIS TOGETHER: THINGS WE WOULD LIKE TO HAVE

Norman Thelwell[99]

Think: Things you aren't necessarily expecting but would be delighted to have and aren't completely impossible to attain if circumstances cooperate. A pony? A convertible? A job based out of the home or that has exotic travel? Twins? Your nose fixed?[100]

PROFESSIONALLY:

Immediately	
5 years	
10 years	
25 years	
Retirement	

RELATIONSHIP-WISE:

Immediately	
5 years	
10 years	
25 years	
Retirement	

It is more important to be wise than right. The relationship is more important than winning the argument. Know when to step back rather than engage. Sometimes it's better to wait to talk until after you've cooled down.

Consider the timing. Don't just dump everything on your [spouse] when he walks in the door. Show that he's valued and respected, give him some time to decompress. (And the conversation may go better if he's not hungry.)

Communication and compromise are key. It's helpful to talk about expectations and plans ahead of time. Don't assume your spouse is a mind reader - you need to tell them what you want. There are less surprises and less stress this way.

Show grace and more grace, again and again. Remember how much you've been forgiven and pass that onto your partner.

There are some great marriage books. I think our favorite is The Marriage Builder by Larry Crab.

The couple that prays together stays together.

Anonymous[101]

Give, and it will be given to you. A good measure, pressed down, shaken together, running over, will be put into your lap; for the measure you give will be the measure you get back. Luke 6:38

DO THIS TOGETHER: WISH LIST

Think: You won the lottery or an unknown rich aunt has left you more than you ever could have imagined or the little book you wrote about marriage becomes an international runaway best seller and literally everyone on the planet buys a copy. Would you … quit your job? Move to Tahiti? Have plastic surgery? Buy a plane? Buy a Lamborghini? Start your own charitable foundation?[102]

PROFESSIONALLY:

RELATIONSHIP-WISE:

> Try not to kill each other.
>
> Boys are way different than girls in many ways.
>
> Get over it ASAP.
>
> John & Linda Arnold[103]

Beloved, let us love one another, because love is from God; everyone who loves is born of God and knows God. I John 4:7

(JUST SOME OF)
SUE'S FAVORITE
BIBLE VERSES

(Yes, I'd be delighted if you looked each one of these up!)

Let all that you do be done in love.

I Corinthians 16:14

- Numbers 6:24-26
- Jeremiah 29:11-14
- Jeremiah 17:7-8
- Hosea 6:3
- I Samuel 16:7b
- Philippians 4:13
- John 3:16
- Deuteronomy 6:5
- Hebrews 11:1
- Isaiah 55:10a
- Zephaniah 3:17

- Romans 10:9
- Colossians 1:15-17
- Philippians 1:20-21
- Romans 8:38-39
- Romans 8:28
- Psalm 18:1-3
- Proverbs 3:5-6
- Isaiah 49:16b
- I Corinthians 14:33
- Galatians 5:22-23
- Ezekiel 36:26
- Psalm 71:5
- 2 Samuel 22:2-4
- Romans 15:13

I PRAY THAT GOD, THE SOURCE OF HOPE, WILL FILL YOU COMPLETELY WITH JOY AND PEACE BECAUSE YOU TRUST IN HIM. THEN YOU WILL OVERFLOW WITH CONFIDENT HOPE THROUGH THE POWER OF THE HOLY SPIRIT.

ROMANS 15:13

The one thing my husband Don and I have lived by is you have to make fun and laughter wherever you are life is short and can be hard you have to grab happiness and joy with all your might. We recently celebrated our 35th wedding anniversary in a rehab facility for my father in law who is fighting bladder cancer. He was having physical therapy and we didn't want to leave him so we turned on Motown music and danced with him in his wheelchair. The memory was priceless. Don't be upset if you are not having a perfect idea of a holiday or celebration the beauty is in the imperfect days filled with love and laughter.

Kim Beavers[104]

Therefore, a man leaves his father and his mother and clings to his wife, and they become one flesh. Genesis 2:24

SUE'S PREFERRED BIBLE TRANSLATIONS

Daq the tagh ghaHta' the mu', je the mu' ghaHta' tlhej joH'a', je the mu' ghaHta' joH'a'.

John 1:1 (In Star Trek Klingon…)[105]

You may wonder what makes a translation a favorite (or not). There are many, many out there and checking out different ones on www.biblegateway.com is a great way to get a good taste.

No one translation is absolutely perfect. Remember that.

For me, I need:

1. **Accuracy.** I want an English translation (from the original Hebrew, Aramaic, and Greek) that does its level best to stay as *true to the original intent of the author* as humanly possible. Even recognizing that this is difficult and not exact, some are definitely better than others.

2. **Inclusive Language.** That means that the Bible translators worked hard to keep the scripture saying *exactly what the original author meant it to say.* So if the original language addressed the direction to

mankind, I want to read "mankind," not "man." I don't want to be part of the "Men-Only" Bible translation club.

<u>Here's an Example</u>: Which do you think has more <u>accurate</u> *and* <u>inclusive</u> language for Genesis 5:2?

- <u>King James Version</u>[106]: "Male and female created he them; and blessed them, and called their name Adam, in the day when they were created."
- <u>New Revised Standard Version</u>: "Male and female he created them, and he blessed them and named them "Humankind"[Hebrew adam] when they were created."

3. **Notes.** I'm delighted to see notes and other study information provided to help me as the reader get the most out of the Scripture as possible. I like to see maps, character profiles, culture notations about societal rules, etc. In the days before "e-copies" this insured that you had a mega-size Bible to lug around. Now, with electronic books, it's so convenient! (Don't ask me how many study Bibles I have on my phone[107].) If this type of information appeals to you, make sure you get a Bible that is specifically labeled as a "Study Bible."

Solid Translations

These translations come directly from original Hebrew, Aramaic, and Greek. Although it is impossible for them to be "word for word" they do their level best to try.

- The New Revised Standard Version [108]
- The New International Version[109]

Paraphrases

Paraphrases are translations that step beyond the "word for word" rule and attempt to reword the Scripture in a manner that makes the text the easiest to read and understand. This involves personal interpretation (to a greater extent) than actual translations.

- The New Living Translation[110]
- The Message[111]
- The Common English Bible[112]

Here's an Example of Genesis 5:2:

- New International Version: "He created them male and female and blessed them. And he named them "Mankind"[Hebrew adam] when they were created."
- New Living Translation: "He created them male and female, and he blessed them and called them "human.""
- The Message: "This is the family tree of the human race: When God created the human race, he made it godlike, with a nature akin to God. He created both male and female and blessed them, the whole human race." (Please note they combine verses 1&2 of Chapter 5 here).
- Common English Bible: "and created them male and female. He blessed them and called them humanity[Hebrew adam]on the day they were created."

"Quit worrying about corroborating your sources—it's not
as if anyone's going to take all this literally."

David Sipress[113]

I never test the water, I just jump in the pool. Joe puts his big toe in and never jumps in until he's tested.

That's how he describes me.

It's not always been easy, but the love has always been there. Amen!

(And never go to sleep angry.)

Barbara Lucas[114]

For God so loved YOU, that He sent His only Son, so that if YOU believe in Him, YOU will not perish but have eternal life. For God did not send His son into the world to condemn YOU, but in order that YOU would be saved. John 3:15-17 (ST)[115]

Mark Streeter[116]

BIBLIOGRAPHY

2004-2016. *Bible Hub.* Accessed March 29, 2019. https://biblehub.com/interlinear/romans/15.htm.

2018. *Blue Letter Bible.* Accessed October 15, 2018. https://www.blueletterbible.org/.

Chambers, Oswald. 1963. *My Utmost For His Highest.* Uhrichsville, OH: Barbour and Company, Inc.

Charleston, Steven. 2015. *The Four Vision Quests of Jesus.* New York: Morehouse Publishing.

2013. *Common English Bible.* Nashville: Common English Bible.

n.d. *Free Dictionary Online.* Accessed July 14, 2019. https://www.thefreedictionary.com/cleave.

Giles, Keith. 2018. *Jesus Unbound: Liberating The Word of God From The Bible.* Orange, California: Quoir.

Harrelson, Walter J., ed. 2003. *The New Interpreter's Study Bible New Revised Standard Version with the Apocrypha.* Nashville: Abingdon Press.

n.d. *https://cyan.com/games/myst/.*

James, Carolyn Custis. 2010. *Hal The Church.* Grand Rapids, MI: Zondervan.

Keller, Tim. 2008. *The Prodigal God.* New York: Riverhead Books.

—. 2008. *The Reason For God.* New York: Riverhead Books.

LeClaire, Jennifer. 2015. *Mornings With The Holy Spirit.* Lake Mary, FL: Charisma.

Lewis, C. S. 2002. *The Complete C.S. Lewis.* San Francisco: Harper.

2011. *New International Version Bible.* Biblica, Inc.

2012. *New Living Translations Study Bible.* Carol Stream, IL: Tyndale House Publishers, Inc.

Peterson, Eugene H. 2002. *The Message.* 2012: Nav Press.

Spangler, Ann, and Jean Syswerda. 1999. *Women of the Bible.* Grand Rapids, MI: Zondervan.

Thurman, Howard. 1996. *Jesus and the Disinherited.* Boston: Beacon Press.

Tozer, A. W. 1943. *The Pursuit of God.* Harrisburg, PA: Christian Publications.

Warren, Rick. 2002. *The Purupose Driven Life.* Grand Rapids, MI: Zondervan.

Yancey, Philip. 2006. *Prayer: Does It Make Any Difference?* Grand Rapids, MI: Zondervan.

For I know the *Plans* I have for you, DECLARES THE LORD

Plans for *Hope* and a *Future.*

Jeremiah 29:11

Life isn't a 50/50 proposition; it's a 100/100 percent proposition.
Live, love, and lean on Christ TOGETHER.

Arlene Hendry[117]

Don't walk away when things get rough.

Have a sense of humor!

Michele Termini[118]

There is no fear in love, but perfect love casts out fear. I John 4:18a

FOOTNOTES & STUFF

I've added some personal bits within this (otherwise often ignored) section. Bless you if you take the time to read them and I hope you maybe laugh out loud once or twice. (Or at least smile.)

---

[1] Art by Maggie Clemmons from the book: Happily Ever After: Stress Relieving Coloring Book,

[2] Tyler Knott Gregson: is a poet, author and professional photographer based in Helena, Montana. Gregson has gained fame as a poet on social media platforms such as Tumblr, Instagram and Twitter since 2009. He writes and posts a "Daily

Haiku on Love," and a raw poem from his "Typewriter Series" every day currently.

[3] (Harrelson 2003) Please note, all scripture referenced in this book is from The New Revised Standard Version unless otherwise specified. 😊

[4] C.S. Lewis is one of my favorite Christian authors. I even taught his entire book, *Mere Christianity*, in pictures!! Some people say he is difficult and deep, when I read him it all made so much sense to me. I love how he gives easy to remember, concrete illustrations for hard, abstract biblical concepts. (That's what 'apologetics' is...!) (If you'd like a free electronic copy of "C.S. Lewis & Me: Mere Christianity in Pictures" just email me at susanmcgeown@faithinspiredbooks.com and I'll send it!!) Here it is on Amazon: https://www.amazon.com/C-S-Lewis-Me-Christianity-Pictures/dp/148180006X/ref=sr_1_2?keywords=c.s.+lewis+in+pictures+susan+mcgeown&qid=1562943738&s=gateway&sr=8-2

[5] If you look up I Samuel 13:14 you will see the account of Samuel the prophet looking for the next king of Israel. God was looking for a man "after His own heart." I remember the first time I read that thinking, "Boy, I'd like to be a woman after God's own heart," and a little voice said, "So what are you waiting for?" Lest you take this the wrong way and think I envision myself to be King or giant-slayer material, I would encourage you to read the entire account of King David's life from start to finish which is hardly stellar. David's best quality was his ability to drag himself back to God, no matter how much he had screwed up, and sincerely beg God's forgiveness... 😊

[6] Amy Grant, Doubly Good, from the album Straight Ahead and Age to Age, January, 1984, Amy Grant Productions. https://www.youtube.com/watch?v=Pz_8WR6gkZ0

[7] This advice was given to me by my dear Father and it is one of the most difficult things to do – at least for me. I have a literal card catalog in my head of slip ups, mistakes, failures, broken promises … for just about everyone I know. Praying about this helps. I cannot tell you how many times God has brought me to a seriously personal insightful moment when I have to hang my head in shame and realize I was the only one in the wrong. Thank you, Lord. ☺

[8] "Paradise By The Dashboard Lights", by Meatloaf, from the album *Bat Out of Hell,* 1977. Don't tell my mother I referenced this song (or that I know it word-for-word by heart!!) ☺
https://www.google.com/search?source=hp&ei=KI0bXbeblrKOggf Emy8&q=meatloaf+paradise+song&oq=meatloaf+paradise&gs_l= psy-
ab.1.5.0l10.586452.590273..594894...0.0..0.254.2013.16j2j2......0. ...1..gws-wiz.....0..0i131.JVxe8SKyfcs

[9] I grew up in a home like this and have raised my children in a home like this. Mom always came first with Dad and I always came first with David. It provides a deep seated stability that is felt on every level of family life. ☺

[10] So, what do you do when you both have a perspective that is 180° out? Someone has to give or the impasse will fester and grow worse. Love, mercy, grace, and understanding is essential between a couple at all times, especially now. David always deferred to me regarding the kids and I always deferred to him regarding financial planning and decisions simply because that's what we both excelled at. All the rest was up for grabs…. ☺

[11] My dear sister in Christ and the first one to respond to my query asking for marriage advice. Married to Mike for 37 years and still going strong!! What I love about Peg is her loyalty, honesty, and commitment towards always Doing The Right Thing. ☺

¹² The Lockhorns, created in 1968 by Bill Hoest and distributed by King Features Syndicate. It continues to be drawn, today, by Bunn Hoest and John Reiner. This was one of my Dad's favorite cartoons. He was forever cutting them out of the paper and sticking them on the refrigerator. ☺

¹³ In our early years of marriage, I was the one who kept quiet and stewed. David finally said, "JUST TELL ME!! THE UNKNOWN IS FAR WORSE THAN THE KNOWN!!!" I've been talking ever since. ☺

¹⁴ I'm one of those people who often gets annoyed/cranky/"out of sorts" before I can articulate what the cause is. Taking the time to figure out why you're acting the way you're acting (especially when you're asked, "What's wrong? You seem upset?") is always wise. My husband has learned to respect the answer, "I don't know. I'm just off. Let me think about it and I'll get back to you." ☺ Me being able to articulate that and him being able to accept that is the sign of a healthy, mature relationship.

¹⁵ Another precious Bible study sister in Christ!! Francine and her guy, Harry, have been married for over 24 years. She told me, "[Harry and I] will be married 24 years in August (2019). I was engaged to [another] high school boy friend of 7 years ... he became friends with another girl ... he broke it off ... they got married and divorced quickly. [Harry and I] married at almost 35 and he was almost 39....made a big difference being mature and financially better..." What I love best about Francine, is she has taught us all, when things get tough to give it to the Lord and then *leave it in His Hands.* Harder than it sounds, this essential peace-of-mind skill becomes easier to do with determination, time, and practice. ☺

¹⁶ I Thessalonians 5:17 Pray without ceasing.

[17] Proverbs 3:5-6 Trust in the Lord with all your heart, and do not rely on your own insight. In all your ways acknowledge Him, and He will make straight your paths.

[18] Early on in our marriage, we started making a list of things we "HAD TO HAVE", "WOULD LIKE TO HAVE", and a "DREAM WISH LIST". We agreed on the list we made and stuck it in the back of the family Bible and committed to pray about it as a couple. We've done this over jobs, big financial purchases, family issues… God has never let us down on this. Not. Once. 🙂

[19] Jeremiah 29:11 For surely I know the plans I have for you, says the LORD, plans for your welfare and not for harm, to give you a future with hope.

[20] Big Black Arrows that the McGeowns have specifically received that turned out to be wonderful blessings in the end (although not at first blush!!): loss of David's job and me having to go back to work to secure health care for the family, failure to be awarded important business contracts, discovery of drug misuse by one of our children, disappointment regarding college acceptances for our children …

Believing that God is in **all** the details, gives you a different perspective in **all** areas of the life!! 🙂

[21] Proverbs 19:21 The human mind may devise many plans, but it is the purpose of the LORD that will be established.

[22] Romans 8:28 We know that all things work together for good for those who love God, who are called according to His purpose. Favorite words in this verse: ALL THINGS.

[23] James 2:23 Thus the scripture was fulfilled that says, "Abraham believed God, and it was reckoned to him as righteous," and he was called the friend of God.

[24] Psalm 119:105: Your word is a lamp to my feet and a light to my path.

[25] Matthew 18:20 For where two or three are gathered in my name, I am there among them.

[26] Galatians 5:22-23 By contrast, the fruit of the Spirit is love, joy, peace, patience, kindness, generosity, faithfulness, gentleness, and self-control. There is no law against such things.

[27] Luke 6:47-49 I will show you what someone is like who comes to me, hears my words, and acts on them. [48] That one is like a man building a house, who dug deeply and laid the foundation on rock; when a flood arose, the river burst against that house but could not shake it, because it had been well built. [49] But the one who hears and does not act is like a man who built a house on the ground without a foundation. When the river burst against it, immediately it fell, and great was the ruin of that house."

[28] Always a Great Read: A. W. Tozer!!

[29] Matthew 7:7 Ask, and it will be given you; search, and you will find; knock, and the door will be opened for you.

[30] Psalm 63:7 For you have been my help, and in the shadow of your wings I sing for joy.

[31] Psalm 106:3 Happy are those who observe justice, who do righteousness at all times.

[32] James 1:17 from the New Living Translation: Whatever is good and perfect is a gift coming down to us from God our Father, who created all the lights in the heavens. He never changes or casts a shifting shadow.

[33] In 1998, my mom collapsed with what turned out to be a brain tumor. Honest to goodness cut-the-top-of-your-skull-off surgery occurred. We were thankful for so many things: wise doctors, kind and caring nurses, health insurance, rapid recovery, and a

benign tumor diagnosis. Plus, now she has a titanium skull top which is bullet proof and who knows when that's going to come in handy, right? 😊

[34] Proverbs 1:7 The fear of the LORD is the beginning of knowledge; fools despise wisdom and instruction.

[35] (Warren 2002)

[36] (Chambers 1963)

[37] (Lewis 2002)

[38] (Keller, The Reason For God 2008)

[39] (LeClaire 2015)

[40] (Charleston 2015)

[41] (Thurman 1996)

[42] (Tozer 1943)

[43] (James 2010)

[44] (Spangler and Syswerda 1999)

[45] (Yancey 2006)

[46] (Keller, The Prodigal God 2008)

[47] (Giles 2018)

[48] My mommy and Daddy married 59 years and 10 months. Daddy went home to be with his Lord last August 13, 2018. 😊

[49] I wrote A PARENT'S TOOLBOX: SURVIVING THE TEEN YEARS but under a pseudonym to protect my family's privacy. (I'm LEE BROOKS!) It's a great how-to-survive booklet that is really misnamed; it works for toddlers, adult children, annoying friends, and wacky relatives, too. Email me at susanmcgeown@faithinspiredbooks.com and I'll send you a free e-copy any time. Here it is on Amazon:

https://www.amazon.com/Parents-Toolbox-Surviving-Teen-Years-ebook/dp/B00EUBFR5I/ref=sr_1_3?keywords=surviving+teen+years+lee+brooks&qid=1562871090&s=gateway&sr=8-3

50 I have no idea who "Jem S" is although I searched high and low on the Internet to find her and give her credit. 😊

51 David and I have regular (excellent) dates at Home Depot (there's a coffee shop nearby), Wegmans Food Stores (they have an eat in area), ... "I'm going to _____. Wanna go on a date with me?" 😊

52 A "grounding" of a teen for one week – no exceptions, firm is more painful than a "grounding" of a teen for "a month" that doesn't last more than a few days. Let your words carry weight, authority, and honesty. 😊

53 This is a drawing by Eloise Wilkin. She illustrates the most beautiful children books. Try to buy one!!! (Search her!!) 😊

54 The Family Circus, by Jeff and Bil Keane, distributed by King Features Syndicate.

55 I made myself walk around the mall and have a frozen yogurt even though I was going through serious withdrawal. I tried to get out once a week and do "me" stuff, it made me a better person all around for everyone involved.

56 https://www.someecards.com/memes/all/

57 Cousin Melanie and Tim have been together for 9 years this November, 2019! 😊

58 Baby Blues is an American comic strip created and produced by Rick Kirkman and Jerry Scott since January 7, 1990. Distributed by King Features Syndicate since 1995, the strip focuses on the MacPherson family and specifically on the raising of the three MacPherson children.

[59] My best girlfriend Linda said to me one time in my early dating career: "You love him, I love him. You hate him, I hate him. Just let me know." *That's* a good friend.

I've known Linda longer than I've known my husband and I will admit that at times I think she understands me better. But her listening, advising, and commiserating *improves* my marriage and life and gives me an improved perspective. We don't always agree but I respect and love her for the strong woman she is. Most importantly, David recognizes her value! Add in Linda's husband, John, who is part of this friendship (and David's wingman in all things 'Sue & Linda') and we are better *as couples* because of this friendship.

[60] I loooove this quote! It's so true. It's thanks to the excellent website www.despair.com. Go ahead. Log on and lose a day laughing your way through the truth of humanity. "Attitudes are contagious. Mine might kill you." Another favorite. LOL. ☺

[61] My sister in Christ, Kris Weigner, and her husband have been married for 50 years and have 3 grown children and one precious

grandchild! Kris' spiritual outlook is a constant source of inspiration for me! 😊

[62] Randy Glasbergen was an American cartoonist and humorous illustrator best known for three decades of newspaper syndication as well as a freelance career. He produced the syndicated strip The Better Half from 1982 to 2014.

[63] My first attempt at meatloaf including adding rice to the mix. I swore my mother used to do it, which she later denied – apparently that was for the meat in her stuffed peppers – and, besides, she used Minute Rice (which cooks in 5 minutes) rather than real rice which after an hour in the oven was still hard. Yes, he ate it. Yes, he said it was good. Yes, I cried. Yes, it made me love him that much more because he is a gourmet cook. 😊

[64] AND a number of babies in dirty diapers AND he had used the good china which I had been told could not go in the dishwasher so, consequently, I swore I would never, ever use it. 😊

[65] Speaking from experience here. At one point three of the five of us were seeing separate counselors. They saved our family. 😊

[66] Think stealing, selling, and taking illegal and prescription drugs, other illegal behavior, sexual proclivities I had never considered, lying and deceit of epic scales, and other things that are still too hard for me to articulate. But we survived and thrived because God has us in the palm of His hand!! 😊

[67] I never say, "I told you so," unless in a previous detailed explanation and warning I said, "AND, when you come back to me in tears and all this has gone to hell, please know that I WILL say, "I told you so," because I live to be able to do that. On the other hand, I welcome the opportunity to be wrong and admit it, which I hope will be the situation this time." WHICH I DO. 😊

68 https://cyan.com/games/myst/

69

https://en.wikipedia.org/wiki/The_Legend_of_Zelda:_Ocarina_of
_Time

70 In the early years of our marriage, we sometimes completely missed the boat with each other. We'd both come home exhausted, each wanted the other to anticipate our Greatest Need (me: favorite chair, a cup of tea, and quality conversation, him: pick up some food at the store so we can have a warm meal with candlelight prepared joyfully side by side). You turn down the dinner, he says he doesn't want a cup of tea and the tiredness turns into anger ("He thinks I want to cook?!" "What the hell am I supposed to eat?!"), disappointment ("Why doesn't he realize I have to *wind down?*" "Does she think I'm going to wait on her?"), frustration ("Why does this always have to happen the first thing when we get home?") Talking about stuff (after she's had a chance to wind down and after he's had a hamburger) regarding how to avoid this repetitive cycle in the future enables you both to not only express what *you* need but hear what *he* needs. A Win-Win. (If you're interested, I became a master at organizing, shopping, ordering, and stocking the food supplies and he often enjoyed preparing dinners – he *likes* to cook! – once he got home.) ☺

71 Tom Vaden, and his girl Laury, have been married 41 years as of June , 2019, and have multiple kids and grandkids, too! Despite the fact that he is not a cat fan, Tom is the kind of guy who you always want to spend time with because he's insightful, entertaining, humble, and downright laugh-out-loud funny. He's been a blessed, God-given friend with his advice on spiritual things, relationship things, and kid things. ☺ (Favorite kid advice: "Boys go up to their room one night at about age 12 and completely transform into some creature that you have no idea

what to do with. But don't worry, they reappear at about age 18 or 19 as terrific human beings. Girls go up to their room one night at about age 11 and completely transform into some creature that you have no idea what to do with. They reappear as terrific human beings any time between ages 25 - 45.")

[72] Copyright Sandra Boynton

[73] https://www.allprodad.com/top-10-things-you-and-your-wife-fight-about/

https://www.bustle.com/articles/165111-the-10-most-common-things-couples-fight-about-according-to-a-sex-therapist

[74] https://www.buzzfeed.com/justinabarca/little-things-couples-inevitably-fight-about

https://www.scarymommy.com/things-couples-argue-about/

[75] If this sounds very ministerial and counselor-atory it should; Todd is actually Rev. Dr. Todd Buurstra and he is the senior pastor at my church, North Branch Reformed Church in Bridgewater, NJ. He also added this sound bit of advice: "I teach couples that one of them is usually a CHASER and the other a SPACER. CHASERS rush to resolve things because they can't stand relational tension. They may be extroverts. SPACERS like to take time to think and don't want to react off the handle to the stress. They may be introverts. Usually heads nod, and they learn that they need each other, and need to learn from each other to balance themselves out. (I'm a chaser, just ask my favorite spacer.)" For me, the friendship was cemented as we sat in his office for the first time and bonded over the desire to empower both our daughters to be/do/become anything they wanted without restriction based on their gender. ☺

[76] Natsuko and Todd Buurstra have been married 36 years. Natsuko has the difficult role of being a mother, a teacher, a wife, *and a senior pastor's wife.* Not something I'd ever want to be!!

Both Natsuko and Todd are dear friends. Their two children matched our two oldest; we even did family vacations together. She said, when she provided me with this, "I did not learn this until later in our marriage and I wish I knew it sooner." 😊

[77] Okay, don't freak out on me, now. Here are the main verses from Genesis – the *first* "marriage ceremony" between the first two humans. I have taken the liberty of going back to the *original Hebrew* to give you clarity on exactly what is stated.

Genesis 1:26-28: Then God said, "Let us make humankind in our image, according to our likeness … So God created humankind in his image, in the image of God he created them; humans [with a penis] and humans [with a vagina]… God blessed them, and God said to them, "Be fruitful and multiply, and fill the earth and subdue it…"

*Genesis 2:18-25: Then the Lord God said, "It is not good [for the human] to be alone; I will make an [equal partner]… So the Lord God caused a deep sleep to fall upon the [human], and as the [human] slept, [God] took [the side of the human] and closed up the place with flesh. And the [side] that the Lord God had taken from the [human] he made into a [second human – 'ishshah'] and brought [ishshah] to the [human]. Then the [human] said, "This at last is bone of my bones and flesh of my flesh; this one shall be called [ishshah] for out of [first human - iysh] this one was taken." Therefore an [male - iysh] leaves father and mother and clings to [female - ishshah], and [those two become one]. And the [human] and the [second human – ishshah – female human] were both naked and were not ashamed. (*This is a "Sue Translation" (ST), a personalized interpretation that I understand for myself whenever I read these verses.)*

A crash course in Hebrew is necessary:

adam (<u>not</u> proper) is the Hebrew word for "human."

zakar is the Hebrew word for "human with a penis."

neqebah is the Hebrew word for "human with a vagina."

ezer kenegdo is Hebrew for "equal partner/warrior."

tsela is the Hebrew word for side/rib/beam.

echad is the Hebrew word for multiple items that have become one – The Trinity is *echad* – three Beings in one. (The Hebrew word *yachid* is for the number one; it is not used here.)

iysh is the term which implies the physical difference that makes one a male human while *ishshah* is the Hebrew term which implies the physical difference that makes one a female human.

[78] *Ishshah* or *ishti* is traditionally translated into "wife." Conversely, there are two words that can be translated into "husband": *ba'al* which is also the term used when referring to an owner of a slave or a master and immediately implies a hierarchy of power (boo-hiss) or *iysh* which is an egalitarian (equal) term which implies simply the physical differences between male and female humans.

[79] Genesis 2:24 states: *"For this reason a [first human - iysh] shall leave [the family head – ab] and his mother [em] and be joined with the [second human - ishshah] and they shall become one flesh."* (This is a "Sue Translation" (ST), a personalized interpretation that I understand for myself whenever I read this verse.)

[80] That's the Hebrew word, *dabaq* if you're wondering which is often translated "cleave" which means (in case you're not sure) "to adhere, cling, or stick fast, to be faithful." (www.thefreedictionary.com)

[81] That's the Hebrew word *azab* which means literally forsake or leave and is paired with the words *ab* and *em* which can mean mother, father, families, clan, tribe chief, humans ... They are

pretty inclusive words that mean "everyone and everything you hold near and dear in your life."

[82] The Hebrew word *hayah* speaks of something "becoming" or "coming to pass" or "happening" or "arising". It's something new and different that the world has never seen before. That's joined with the Hebrew words *echad* which has a spiritual kind of quality to it in that it means "many becoming one" or "only, once and for all" *basar* which means literally "skin" or "body" or "blood relations" all of which have connections that cannot be separated without death occurring.

[83] Genesis 1:26-28 states: Then God said, *"Let us make humankind in our image, according to our likeness; and let them have dominion over the fish of the sea, and over the birds of the air, and over the cattle, and over all the wild animals of the earth, and over every creeping thing that creeps upon the earth."*

[27] So God created humankind in his image,
  in the image of God he created them;
  male and female he created them.

[28] God blessed them, and God said to them, "Be fruitful and multiply, and fill the earth and subdue it; and have dominion over the fish of the sea and over the birds of the air and over every living thing that moves upon the earth." *[29] God said, "See, I have given you every plant yielding seed that is upon the face of all the earth, and every tree with seed in its fruit; you shall have them for food. [30] And to every beast of the earth, and to every bird of the air, and to everything that creeps on the earth, everything that has the breath of life, I have given every green plant for food." And it was so. [31] God saw everything that he had made, and indeed, it was very good.* (NRSV)

[84] A blessing is "divine favor", "to confer well-being or prosperity on", "to endow as with talent" (www.thefreedictionary.com)

[85] The Hebrew word *parah* means to "bear fruit" or "branch off" and the Hebrew word *rabah* (not to be confused with radah below!!) means to "become great" or "become many" or "be numerous" or "grow great" or "increase"...

[86] The Hebrew word *radah* means "to rule", "have dominion", "dominate" ...

[87] (FYI: I list Mark 10 *before* Matthew 19 – even though Matthew shows up first in the Bible – because it is believed that Mark was actually written *before* Matthew!)

Teaching about Divorce (NRSV)

Mark 10 He left that place and went to the region of Judea and beyond the Jordan. And crowds again gathered around him; and, as was his custom, he again taught them.

[2] Some Pharisees came, and to test him they asked, "Is it lawful for a man to divorce his wife?" [3] He answered them, "What did Moses command you?" [4] They said, "Moses allowed a man to write a certificate of dismissal and to divorce her." [5] But Jesus said to them, "Because of your hardness of heart he wrote this commandment for you. [6] But from the beginning of creation, 'God made them male and female.' [7] 'For this reason a man shall leave his father and mother, [8] and the two shall become one flesh.' So they are no longer two, but one flesh. [9] Therefore what God has joined together, let no one separate."

[10] Then in the house the disciples asked him again about this matter. [11] He said to them, "Whoever divorces his wife and marries another commits adultery against her; [12] and if she divorces her husband and marries another, she commits adultery."

What Jesus Taught about Marriage and Divorce (NRSV)

Matthew 19 When Jesus had finished talking, He went from the country of Galilee. He came to the part of the country of Judea which is on the other side of the Jordan River. ² Many people followed Him and He healed them there.

³ The proud religious law-keepers came to Jesus. They tried to trap Him by saying, "Does the Law say a man can divorce his wife for any reason?" ⁴ He said to them, "Have you not read that He Who made them in the first place made them man and woman? ⁵ It says, 'For this reason a man will leave his father and his mother and will live with his wife. The two will become one.' ⁶ So they are no longer two but one. Let no man divide what God has put together."

⁷ The proud religious law-keepers said to Jesus, "Then why did the Law of Moses allow a man to divorce his wife if he put it down in writing and gave it to her?" ⁸ Jesus said to them, "Because of your hard hearts Moses allowed you to divorce your wives. It was not like that from the beginning. ⁹ And I say to you, whoever divorces his wife, except for sex sins, and marries another, is guilty of sex sins in marriage. Whoever marries her that is divorced is guilty of sex sins in marriage."

¹⁰ His followers said to Him, "If that is the way of a man with his wife, it is better not to be married." ¹¹ But Jesus said to them, "Not all men are able to do this, but only those to whom it has been given. ¹² For there are some men who from birth will never be able to have children. There are some men who have been made so by men. There are some men who have had themselves made that way because of the holy nation of heaven. The one who is able to do this, let him do it."

What Jesus Taught about Adultery/Infidelity (NRSV)

John 8 [1] while Jesus went to the Mount of Olives. [2] Early in the morning he came again to the temple. All the people came to him and he sat down and began to teach them. [3] The scribes and the Pharisees brought a woman who had been caught in adultery; and making her stand before all of them, [4] they said to him, "Teacher, this woman was caught in the very act of committing adultery. [5] Now in the law Moses commanded us to stone such women. Now what do you say?" [6] They said this to test him, so that they might have some charge to bring against him. Jesus bent down and wrote with his finger on the ground. [7] When they kept on questioning him, he straightened up and said to them, "Let anyone among you who is without sin be the first to throw a stone at her." [8] And once again he bent down and wrote on the ground.[a] [9] When they heard it, they went away, one by one, beginning with the elders; and Jesus was left alone with the woman standing before him. [10] Jesus straightened up and said to her, "Woman, where are they? Has no one condemned you?" [11] She said, "No one, sir."[b] And Jesus said, "Neither do I condemn you. Go your way, and from now on do not sin again."

[88] **_Jesus' Great Commission_**: Matthew 28:18-20 NRSV *And Jesus came and said to them, "All authority in heaven and on earth has been given to me. [19] Go therefore and make disciples of all nations, baptizing them in the name of the Father and of the Son and of the Holy Spirit, [20] and teaching them to obey everything that I have commanded you. And remember, I am with you always, to the end of the age."*

[89] Mary the mother of Jesus and her cousin Elizabeth were filled with the Holy Spirit from the start! Read Luke 1:26-45!

[90] Acts 1:14 (RSV) *"All these were constantly devoting themselves to prayer, together with certain women, including Mary the mother of Jesus, as well as his brothers."*

[91] Ephesians 5:21-33 (NRSV) **_The Christian Household_**

[21] Be subject to one another out of reverence for Christ.

22 Wives, be subject to your husbands as you are to the Lord. 23 For the husband is the head of the wife just as Christ is the head of the church, the body of which he is the Savior. 24 Just as the church is subject to Christ, so also wives ought to be, in everything, to their husbands.

25 Husbands, love your wives, just as Christ loved the church and gave himself up for her, 26 in order to make her holy by cleansing her with the washing of water by the word, 27 so as to present the church to himself in splendor, without a spot or wrinkle or anything of the kind—yes, so that she may be holy and without blemish. 28 In the same way, husbands should love their wives as they do their own bodies. He who loves his wife loves himself. 29 For no one ever hates his own body, but he nourishes and tenderly cares for it, just as Christ does for the church, 30 because we are members of his body. 31 "For this reason a man will leave his father and mother and be joined to his wife, and the two will become one flesh." 32 This is a great mystery, and I am applying it to Christ and the church. 33 Each of you, however, should love his wife as himself, and a wife should respect her husband.

92 Queen Victoria and Prince Albert were married on January 25, 1858.

93 Love Cathy Thorne cartoons. Everyday People is a cartoon written and drawn by Cathy Thorne. The cartoon generally uses a single captioned panel featuring a female protagonist. The series debuted in 1999, and has been in continuous production ever since, publishing a new cartoon on a weekly schedule.
https://everydaypeoplecartoons.com/

94 Another blessed sister in Christ. Sue and her husband, John, have 2 children and will have been married for 30 years this coming March, 2020. Sue has such a heart for others and has

taught me to listen, love, and accept. Whenever she speaks, I listen closely!! 😊

[95] Robin and her husband, Craig, have been married for 31 years and have 3 grown children. Another sister in Christ (I'm blessed with a lot of sisters, aren't I?!). What I love about Robin is she is a true example of someone who not only "talks the talk" but "walks the walk"!! 😊

[96] Henry Payne is an American editorial cartoonist for The Detroit News. Payne began cartooning when he was a student at Princeton University, drawing for two of its student publications, The Daily Princetonian and The Nassau Weekly.

[97] Our Have-To-Have wish list originally was: a salary that would enable me to stay home (comfortably) with the children, health insurance, an opportunity to start a 401k… Later we added things like if substantial business travel was involved then non-travel business time was in a home office. When we started our own business, we added a salary large enough that enabled us to pay for our own health insurance… 😊

[98] Yes, this is my hubby. We will hit 28 years together on July 20, 2019. We are the proud parents of 3 biological children and one very precious "adopted" young man (he's mine, you can't have him!). Some of David's advice is already stated in my Top Ten Advice list. Father Murphy told us about the renewing the vows every day when we had the blessing of our marriage in England on August 3, 1991. "Happiness is being married to your best friend" is a plaque that hangs on our bedroom wall and what we faithfully write in every wedding card we sign. The submitting to your wife crack … I know he was joking as we have an egalitarian marriage (we fully embrace Ephesians 5:21 which says *"Be subject to one another out of reverence for Christ."*) and I suspect he had no idea that this was going to show up in a book. LOL. 😊

[99] My sister always wanted a pony. She still does. And she's serious. This is a drawing of a Thelwell Pony!! Thelwell is regarded as the unofficial artist of the British countryside and is possibly the most popular cartoonist in Britain, since the Second World War. He commented on many aspects of human behavior, but he is perhaps most synonymous with little girls and their little fat ponies. They have helped to ensure his continuing popularity and his immortality. http://www.thelwell.org.uk/ ☺

[100] Our "Have to Have" list was so carefully thought out that this list was actually kind of difficult for us and, if I'm being honest here, I don't think we ever attained much on this list but didn't care!! Things like a company car, keeping travel miles/points so we could use them for personal things, commuting expenses paid for or supplemented by employer, matching 401k account by employer, would show up on this list. ☺

[101] I couldn't get my wise friend to take credit. I dearly love the entire family; they have richly blessed my life and my family in more words than I can express. ☺

[102] David has always wanted his own plane (yes, seriously) and that has remained as the only thing on his list. I'd like a zippy convertible sports car with a 6-speed manual transmission like my old Mazda RX-7 but my current Mini Cooper sport is almost as nice!!! And maybe to becoming a best-selling author but only if it's the Lord's will. ☺

[103] I love these two dearly!!! We are godparents to each other's children and I have been a part of Linda and John Arnold's life longer than I've been married to my husband. Married for 38 years, they met in college and have one daughter (MY GODDAUGHTER), Jayne Lynn. My favorite thing about them is that they know each other so well that they can finish each other's sentences and anticipate each other's needs telepathically. And, they both have a fabulous sense of humor.

The "Don't Kill Each Other" was a private vow they made to each other at the start of their marriage. (Snicker.) 😊

[104] What fantastic advice!! Kim is right! Kim is a blessed, new sister in Christ. If you wait for things to be "perfect" or "just like you want them" to be happy and enjoy the moment you will never find enjoyment in life. We call this, "Making lemonade out of lemons!!" 😊

[105] I searched "funny translations of the Bible and came up with an honest to goodness Klingon Language Version of the World English Bible. John 1:1 (in English) states, "In the beginning was the Word, and the Word was with God, and the Word was God." http://crosswire.org/study/parallelstudy.jsp?del=all&key=John&add=KLV&add=NASB http://mentalfloss.com/article/52016/4-unusual-bible-translations 😊

[106] In 1604, King James I of England authorized that a new translation of the Bible into English be started. It was finished in 1611, just 85 years after the first translation of the New Testament into English appeared (Tyndale, 1526). The Authorized Version, or King James Version, quickly became the standard for English-speaking Protestants. Its flowing language and prose rhythm has had a profound influence on the literature of the past 400 years. The King James Version present on the Bible Gateway matches the 1987 printing. The KJV is public domain in the United States.

[107] Okay, so you asked. I have eight! (LOL, Even I'm a little surprised at that number!): The New Revised Standard Version Cultural Background Bible, the New Living Translation Study Bible, The Common English Study Bible, The New Oxford Annotated New Revised Standard Version Study Bible, the New International Study Bible, the New Living Translation Life Application Study Bible, the English Stand Version Study Bible, and the Jewish Study Bible. 😊

[108] (Harrelson 2003)

[109] (New International Version Bible 2011)

[110] (New Living Translations Study Bible 2012)

[111] (Peterson 2002)

[112] (Common English Bible 2013)

[113] David Sipress's first cartoon appeared in *The New Yorker* in 1998. During the 2012 Presidential election, he was newyorker.com's first daily cartoonist. His work has also appeared in the Boston *Phoenix*, *Time*, *Parade*, *Playboy*, *Funny Times*, the Washington *Post*, *Harper's*, *Gastronomica*, and *Shambhala Sun*. Sipress has lectured on the art of the cartoon, and he was the writer and host of "Conversations with Cartoonists," a series of onstage interviews with many of the artists who contribute to *The New Yorker*. Sipress has contributed both fiction and nonfiction to *The New Yorker*, including "A Nineteen-Fifties Jewish-American Christmas Story," on how his family celebrated Hanukkah and Christmas simultaneously, and "How to Survive as a Cartoonist in Trumpland." https://www.newyorker.com/contributors/david-sipress

[114] Barbara and Joe Lucas have been married 58 years! They are proud parents, grandparents multiple times over. I enjoy how connected they always seem to be and yet how independent they both are as well. 😊

[115] This is a "Sue Translation" (ST), a personalized interpretation that I read for myself whenever I think of this precious verse. Here it is in the New Revised Standard Version: John 3:16-17 *For God so loved the world that He gave His only Son, so that everyone who believes in Him may not perish but may have eternal life. Indeed, God did not send the Son into the world to*

condemn the world, but in order that the world might be saved through Him. 😊

[116] Mark Streeter Cartoons Mark Streeter is the staff cartoonist for the Savannah Morning News.
https://www.cagle.com/author/mark-streeter/

[117] Arlene is another dear sister in Christ. She and her husband, Dave, were married for 42 years and were blessed with 2 daughters. Her life is now full enjoying time with her grandchildren! Arlene's parents, Arthur and Kathleen Jenssen are still going strong at SEVENTY-THREE years together and embrace the same attitude and advice!!! 😊

[118] Michele, another dear sister in Christ sent a funny video along with her advice – I wish I could share it!! 😊

Below: Pickles comic strip, Pickles is a daily and Sunday comic strip by Brian Crane focusing on a retired couple in their seventies, Earl and Opal Pickles. Pickles has been published since April 2, 1990. It was my dad's favorite!!

Brian Crane

www.ingramcontent.com/pod-product-compliance
Lightning Source LLC
Chambersburg PA
CBHW051043030426
42339CB00006B/176